Meet the Meerkat

Darrin Lunde

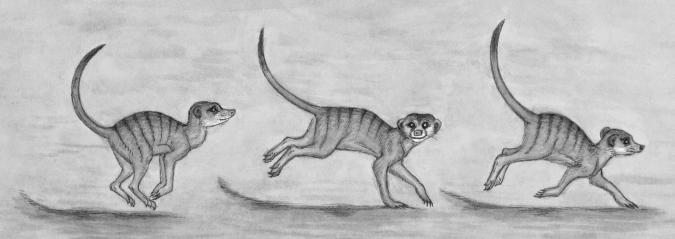

Illustrated by

Patricia J. Wynne

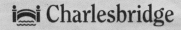 Charlesbridge

Hello, little animal.
What is your name?

My name is Little Meerkat.

I am a kind of mongoose.

Little Meerkat,
what do you look like?

I am long and thin.

I have a pointy face.

I am the size of a squirrel.

Little Meerkat,
where do you live?

I live in the African desert.

I like the hot sun.

Little Meerkat,
do you live alone?

I live with my brothers and sisters.

We all live in the same den.

Little Meerkat, what do you do all day?

In the morning I warm up in the sun.

Then I run with my brothers
and sisters to find food.

Little Meerkat,
what do you eat?

I eat insects, spiders, and scorpions.

I smell them with my nose.

Then I dig them up with my feet.

Little Meerkat,
do you make any sounds?

I make funny sounds all day long.

Cluck . . . *murmur, murmur* . . . *peep!*

I say *waauk-waauk* when

   I see something dangerous.

Little Meerkat,
what do you fear?

I am afraid of eagles and jackals.

These animals try to eat me.

I take turns with my brothers and sisters

  to watch for danger.

Little Meerkat,
when do you sleep?

I return to my den just before dark.

Good night, Little Meerkat!

Meerkats do not like cold mornings.

They are most active during the warm part of the day.

There is not much food where meerkats live.

They have to travel far to find enough to eat.

Meerkats live in groups of ten or more.

They like to be around other meerkats.

They care for other meerkats who are sick or hurt.

They sometimes even hug each other.

For my lovely wife, Sakiko—D. L.

For Donald, alert as ever—P. J. W.

Text copyright © 2007 by Darrin Lunde
Illustrations copyright © 2007 by Patricia J. Wynne

Published by Charlesbridge
85 Main Street
Watertown, MA 02472
(617) 926-0329
www.charlesbridge.com

Library of Congress Cataloging-in-Publication Data
Lunde, Darrin P.
    Meet the Meerkat / Darrin Lunde ; illustrated by Patricia J. Wynne.
        p. cm.
    ISBN 978-1-58089-110-3 (reinforced for library use)
    ISBN 978-1-58089-154-7 (softcover)
1. Meerkat—Juvenile literature. I. Wynne, Patricia, ill. II. Title.
QL737.C235L86 2007
599.74'2—dc22   2006021252

Printed in China
(hc) 10 9 8 7 6 5 4 3 2 1
(sc) 10 9 8 7 6 5 4 3 2 1

Illustrations done in watercolor, ink, and colored pencil
Display type and text type set in Billy from SparkyType
Color separations by Chroma Graphics, Singapore
Printed and bound by Regent Publishing Services
Production supervision by Brian G. Walker
Designed by Susan Mallory Sherman